Baby's Guide to RAISING MOM

Crib Notes For Bringing Up Parents

R.J. Fischer

PINNACLE BOOKS
http://www.pinnaclebooks.com

PINNACLE BOOKS are published by

Kensington Publishing Corp.
850 Third Avenue
New York, NY 10022

Pinnacle and the P logo Reg. U.S. Pat. & TM Off.

First Printing: May, 1997
10 9 8 7 6 5 4 3 2 1

Printed in the United States of America

This book is dedicated to Iris,
who's about to experience all this for herself.

If you're doing something cute, and Mommy gets the camera, stop right before she can take the picture. When she puts the camera away, do something cute again.

Wiggle when Mommy tries to diaper you—she needs the challenge.

Never play with a toy more than once.

When Mommy takes you visiting, identify the most fragile thing in the house and head straight for it.

Stay up late and sleep during the day.

When Mommy feeds you, spit out your food. When Daddy feeds you, eat it all and then smile.

Make sure you say "Da-Da" at least a month before you say "Ma-Ma."

If Mommy takes you to day care, scream until she leaves. A little parental guilt is a good thing.

Ask to hear the same story every night, over and over.

Give the dog your food.

Never go to bed without a struggle.

Scream in terror when Mommy takes you to see Santa.

Take your first steps when Mommy's out of film.

Ask for a glass of water at bedtime, then spill it so Mommy
has to change the sheets.

Regard all baby-sitters as enemies.

If Mommy forgets to put a towel over her shoulder when she burps you, be sure to spit up. She'll remember next time.

When Mommy dresses you in a new outfit, get it dirty right away.

Always cry loudly in church.

Make sure that you need a new diaper whenever there's no convenient place to change you.

Refuse to sit in your car seat.

Bang on your highchair tray during all meals.

At bedtime, pretend to go to sleep. Cry when Mommy
tries to tiptoe out of the room.

Throw your spoon on the floor and see how many times
Mommy will pick it up.

11

See how many times you can get Mommy to jump up
during a meal. She needs the exercise.

Tug on Mommy's earrings. She shouldn't wear them
around you, anyway.

Splash when Mommy gives you a bath. She needs one,
too.

It's a proven fact that food is more tasty if you get it all over your face.

Be a finicky eater and you'll get better stuff.

Learn to crawl faster than Mommy can run.

Help Mommy keep the house neat by throwing everything off the coffee table at least once a day.

Refuse to learn the difference between "yes" and "no."

The bars on your crib are designed for baby aerobics. Learn to pull yourself up and climb out.

If Mommy leaves breakable items where you can reach them, teach her to be more careful.

Fall asleep in your baby swing, but wake up the minute Mommy takes you out and tries to put you in your crib.

Mealtime is fun. Play with your food.

Demand two cookies, one for each hand.

Throw your rattle and see how many times Mommy will retrieve it. If it's less than twenty, scream.

Learn the names of things around the house. (Hint: if you want to play with it, it's probably a "no-no.")

When Mommy puts her finger in your mouth to check for a new tooth, bite down hard to show her you have one.

The mattress in your crib is a baby trampoline. Practice jumping on it every day.

Don't fall for the old "distract the baby with a toy" trick.

Crawl into tight places where Mommy can't reach you.

Squeeze the nipple on your bottle so it squirts out milk.

Mommy will be very proud when you take your first steps. When she tries to show Daddy, pretend you forgot how to do it.

Never admit that you're potty-trained.

Learn to open the refrigerator and get out the eggs.
They're fun to crack on the floor.

Flour and water make paste.

When Mommy asks what you're doing, always say "nothing."

Learn how to unplug the phone.

Say you like the food better at Grandma's house.

When Mommy asks if you'd like a new baby brother or sister, say you'd rather have a puppy.

Learn to turn on the water faucets by yourself.

Tell Mommy the baby-sitter was mean to you.

If Mommy takes you to a restaurant, throw the silverware.

Learn to flush the toilet and do it constantly.

Decorate Mommy's walls with your crayons. She loves the pictures you draw.

Crackers are fun to crumble. Make sure you get them all over the carpet.

Pretend you're terrorized by the vacuum cleaner.

Practice turning blue in the face when Mommy says you can't have another cookie.

If you're out in public, and you have to go to the potty, announce it to everyone in a loud, clear voice.

Be very messy when Mommy feeds you beets.

Take little naps during the day so you can stay up really late.

28

Kick when Mommy tries to tie your shoes. She'll buy you new ones with Velcro fasteners.

Learn to untie your bib when Mommy's not looking.

Never believe that stupid old saying that children should be seen but not heard.

If you use your imagination, you can find lots of things to do with spaghetti.

Don't tell Mommy you have to go to the potty until she gets you all dressed up in your snowsuit.

Listen for the phrase, "Be a big boy," or "Be a big girl." It usually precedes something very unpleasant.

Correct Mommy if she tries to skip part of your favorite bedtime story. Then make her read it all over again from the beginning.

Warning: If Mommy says something is good for you, you're not going to like it.

Force Mommy to take a spoonful before she feeds you. If she makes a face, don't eat it.

Never admit that you have to go to the potty until after Mommy puts you in your car seat.

Don't be fooled. The food in your little bowl is never as good as the food on Mommy or Daddy's plate.

Learn to wiggle out of your diaper when nature calls.

Mommy will try to teach you to blow your nose. Do it, but jerk back quickly before she can wipe with the tissue.

Remember that fingers were here before spoons or forks, and they're a lot easier to use.

33

After Mommy gives you a bottle, burp very loudly. For some reason, parents seem to like that.

When you wake up in the morning, don't stay in your crib and play with your toys. Mommy will want to know the second you're awake.

Teach Mommy to leave a night light on in your room by screaming at the dark. That way no one will trip when they come in to check on you.

Cry when Mommy picks you up at day care. She'll feel guilty that she's taking you away from your friends, and she'll play with you for several hours.

Learn how to spell and don't tell Mommy or Daddy. You'll discover exactly what you're getting for Christmas.

When Mommy teaches you a song, sing it over and over for her. She'll be so happy you were paying attention.

Make sure you talk louder than anyone else in the room.

Resist potty-training and Mommy will spend hours of quality time in the bathroom with you.

French fries are better if you squish them first.

Learn to drool on everyone who holds you.

Never eat baby food if you can reach Mommy or Daddy's plate.

Eat the bottom part of the cone first, so the ice cream will dribble out.

Show Mommy she was wrong about the things she thought were unbreakable.

If something is tied, untie it.

If something is zipped, unzip it.

If something is locked, scream.

All food is finger food, even soup.

Daddy loves a treasure hunt. Hide the TV remote control.

Be sure to make lots of noise when Mommy's on the phone.

If something is "out of reach," it's a challenge.

Make Mommy carry you when her arms are full.

Learn to answer the phone when it rings. When the person on the line says, "Hello? Hello?" hang up.

Grocery shopping is fun. Help Mommy by putting things in the cart when she isn't looking.

Refuse to walk when you can be carried.

Highchair trays can make lots of noise if you bang on them with your spoon.

If Mommy gives you a glass cup, throw it on the floor. It'll teach her to use plastic.

When you pull the bottom can out of a grocery store display, the other cans will make a big noise.

Show Mommy that your full cereal bowl can be used as a hat.

Make Mommy hold you when she's writing a check at the store.

43

Everyone says that a milk bath is good for the skin.

Food is colorful and looks nice on the wall.

Teach Mommy to be a circus performer by making her juggle three bags of groceries and you.

If you bang your feet against the footrest on the stroller,
it'll sound like a drum.

Prepare for a future in baseball. Learn to throw toys at
a moving target, preferably Mommy.

"No" always means "maybe" unless it's shouted.

Snow is more fun if you put some down Mommy's neck.

Play hide-and-seek with Mommy, and don't come out until there are lots of people with uniforms in the house.

Fall asleep the second they put you in the stroller at Disneyland. When you're back in the car, on the way home, cry because you didn't get to see Mickey Mouse.

Mommy's lipstick is just like a crayon. Teach her to keep it out of reach in a drawer.

Shake every present under the Christmas tree until it makes some kind of noise.

If Mommy says something is a "naughty" word, make sure to remember it for later.

Rearrange all the things in Daddy's desk. It'll teach him to lock the drawers.

Teach Mommy that if something falls on the floor, it's yours.

Furniture is meant for climbing.

If you hear the phrase, "Little pitchers have big ears," listen very carefully to whatever follows.

Teach Mommy that parents shouldn't have white carpeting.

Turn up the volume on the morning cartoons if you want Mommy to get out of bed and make you breakfast.

If someone says, "Not in front of the baby," pay close attention.

There are lots of fun things in the trash. Convince Mommy to buy a covered wastebasket for the kitchen.

Cats make funny noises when you pull on their tails.

A balloon will go bang if you pinch it hard. Take it to Daddy, ask him to fix it, and he'll go out to buy more.

The dog is your friend. If you drop the food you don't like on the floor, he'll eat it before Mommy notices.

If you break your balloon and then cry, you can watch Mommy's face turn red when she blows up another one.

Cry until they let the dog sleep in your room. A warm, furry friend in your bed is a wonderful comfort.

If Mommy has long fingernails, scream when she diapers you. After a few reminders, she'll cut them short.

Insist that Mommy put all of your floating toys in the bathtub at once.

Always remember to scream when you play.

If you do something naughty, blame it on your imaginary playmate. Mommy will think it's clever . . . for a while.

Practice pouting in front of the mirror. There's no limit to what Mommy will do to make you smile again.

Learn to cry real tears on demand.

If you make enough suds with the bubble bath, Mommy won't be able to find you.

If Mommy foolishly leaves out a dish of chocolates, squeeze each piece to find the one you like.

After squeezing the chocolates, wipe your hands off on the drapes.

If you want Mommy to worry, do exactly what she says all day long.

Mashed potatoes make an excellent medium for sculpture.

Teach Mommy never to leave you alone in the car for even a minute by locking all the doors so she can't get back in.

Boys only: When you're out in public and you have to go potty, make sure Mommy takes you.

Girls only: When you're out in public and you have to go potty, make sure Daddy takes you.

Be creative. There are over a hundred uses for dirt.

If you want to see Mommy shudder, make the reptile house your favorite part of the zoo.

If you climb to the very top of the jungle gym, Mommy won't be able to get you down.

The backseat of the car makes a great trampoline.

Mommy will turn green if you make her take you on the merry-go-round enough times in a row.

If the baby-sitter says it's bedtime, refuse to believe her.

Babies need much less sleep-time than Mommies.

Don't fall for the old nap ploy. A nap is only an excuse for Mommy to have fun without you.

You can help Mommy stay in shape if you make her push you on the swing for hours.

Find out what Mommy and Daddy do when they think you're asleep.

Make Mommy look silly. Pretend that you're afraid to go on the slide alone.

Get your days and nights mixed up.

Babies need more color in their lives. Spill things that stain.

Drive Mommy crazy. If you liked something yesterday, pretend to hate it today.

There's always mud somewhere on a playground.

Never let Mommy sit for more than five minutes at the park. She took you there to play, didn't she?

Always fall asleep five minutes before the car stops, so you're really cranky when you wake up.

Mommies like to do laundry. Contribute at least two washer loads every day.

If you repeat the phrase, "What's that?" over and over, it will make Mommy's face turn red.

Take little naps during the day, so you're alert and active when nighttime rolls around.

Everybody says that TV rots the mind. Never let Mommy watch a complete program.

It's okay to fall asleep in your stroller, but if Mommy stops pushing, wake up and protest.

If you put toy cars under Mommy's feet, she may do some fancy acrobatics for you.

Never eat wholesome food when you can have snacks.

"Why" is a fun question. Ask it after Mommy tells you something. When she answers, ask it again. This little game can go on for hours.

Scream loudly if Mommy has to undress you to change
your diaper. She'll buy baby outfits with snaps on the
legs.

Never sleep in a bed if there's an available lap.

Babies have sharp elbows. Use them to climb Mommy
when she's holding you.

There are lots of neat things buried in the fibers of the carpet. Find them all.

The mattress in a car bed is never more comfortable than Mommy's arms.

If you pile lots of things on the sofa, you can stand up on them.

The pedals on a tricycle rotate both ways. Learn to go backward when Mommy's standing behind you.

If you pretend that you're afraid to ride your tricycle alone, Mommy will push you, and you won't have to pedal.

Make sure you can run backward much faster than
Mommy can run forward.

Chairs are not just for sitting. They make dandy ramps
for jumping.

Clothes cause wind resistance. You can run faster if you're
naked.

Practice saying "no" over and over in a loud, authoritative voice.

Teach Mommy that baby walkers are unsafe by banging into her ankles.

There's more to a parade than people's legs. Make Mommy lift you up so you can see.

"Horsie" is a good game to strengthen Daddy's back muscles. Make him play it the minute he comes home from work.

Mommy will tell you that the doctor is a nice man. Don't buy it.

If you want to see Daddy's face turn purple, pull on his tie and don't let go.

Play with a toy in the toy store. When Mommy buys it
and brings it home, refuse to touch it.

If the doctor promises you that it won't hurt, it's time to
scream.

Show Mommy how many things are breakable in the
store.

If someone you don't like tries to pick you up, make your whole body as stiff as a board.

If you really stretch, you can reach the spigot on the bottled-water cooler. It's a good way to show Mommy how tall you've grown.

When in doubt, squirm.

If you spill sugar, all the ants will come in to see you.

If Mommy dresses you up in a silly outfit, spill something on it right away.

When Mommy takes you to baby classes, don't let her talk to any of the other Mommies. They may have ideas that will make your life less fun.

If you tug very hard, you can pull Mommy's clothes off the hangers.

The big day has come. Mommy gives you your first peanut butter and jelly sandwich. Squeeze it to make sure she put in enough jelly.

With a spoon for a catapult, you can hurl globs of chocolate pudding.

You can see exactly where the kitty walks if you put peanut butter on her paws.

Learn to use your fork wisely. With a little practice, you can reach out to spear French fries from Daddy's plate.

Mommy is wrong. Couch cushions belong on the floor.

If you crawl under a lady's dress, she might scream.

Peanut butter makes an excellent paste.

If you chew on the remote control, you can change the
channels all by yourself.

Pour honey all over the floor, so the dog can have some.

Mommy says cats like milk. Pour some on Fluffy.

Ask Mommy to help you put the toothpaste back in the tube.

Anything you can pick up can be thrown.

Show Mommy that there are feathers inside your pillow.

Demand paper money from the Tooth Fairy.

Daddy's computer will make a funny noise if you turn it on and off really fast.

Find out what's inside your stuffed toys.

A rock makes a big noise if you throw it at a window.

CD's are like Frisbees. Practice throwing them.

If something has a rip, make it bigger.

Learn to unbutton clothes by yourself. When someone holds you, unbutton every button you can reach.

Velcro makes a funny noise when you tear it open. Do it over and over.

Mommy will do almost anything to keep you on the potty chair.

Most things will bounce down the stairs if you throw them hard enough.

Birthday parties are fun only if you can open the presents.

Empty Mommy's purse on the floor. You never know what treasures you might find.

Toys are more fun if they belong to someone else.

If you don't feel like walking, sit down and whimper.
Someone will be sure to carry you.

Bath time is only fun if Mommy gets wet, too.

If you practice very hard, you can climb the drapes.

Contrary to what Mommy may tell you, there is no such thing as a child who's too big to carry.

Practice the art of the full-scale tantrum. It can get you almost anything you want.

When Mommy rakes the leaves in a pile, put them back where they belong.

If you turn on the bathroom faucet all the way, the water will splash out on the floor.

Tissues make lots of little white balls if you put them in the washing machine.

Jump on Mommy in the middle of the night to show her that you can get out of your crib all by yourself.

Learn to pull off your wet diapers and hide them as a surprise for Mommy.

Baby powder looks like snow if you sprinkle it on the rug.

Mommy will be so happy if you say "please" and "thank you," she'll give you almost anything you want.

Cry loudly and the baby-sitter will give you anything you want.

If all else fails, hold your breath until you turn blue.

Bring lots of snow inside to play with later.

You'll be sure to regret it if you let Mommy take a picture
of you naked, on a bearskin rug.

All banisters are designed for sliding.

Tell Mommy you saw a big mousie, even if you didn't.

Never nap for more than five minutes at a time.

Practice counting to ten, over and over, whenever Mommy's balancing her checkbook.

The newspaper is fun to tear, especially before Mommy's read it.

Those little knobs in the back of the TV make the picture jump up and down.

You can hide lots of things in the vacuum cleaner hose.

If something won't fit in something else, squish it until it does.

Ice cubes are fun to play with.

If you sit on Daddy's Xerox machine, it'll take a nice picture of your bottom.

Never color in the same place twice.

If you scrunch up a piece of bread, it'll fit in one hand.

Roll down your window when Mommy takes you through the car wash. The inside of the car should get clean, too.

Grandmas are always good for another cookie.

Even M&M's melt if you hold them in your hand long enough.

Mommy will scream if you put a bug in her glass.

Bring Mommy that wonderful dead lizard you found.

Practice splashing in puddles until you can get everyone around you wet.

Mud is even better than modeling clay.

When someone tosses you up in the air, express your disapproval by throwing up on them.

A swivel chair can be a merry-go-round.

Water beds can turn into geysers if you poke them with something sharp.

Make sure you lose one mitten from every pair. Mommy will buy the clips that attach them to your sleeves.

There's no limit to the number of things that you can flush down the toilet.

There are lots of creative ways to sit on a chair.

Make sure you hide a crayon in your hand if Mommy makes you sit in a corner.

Teach Mommy that sending you to your room when you're naughty doesn't mean you'll be good when she lets you out.

When Mommy takes you to the photographer, refuse to smile.